YOUR QUESTIONS

OUR ANSWERS

Dear Chris:

Prayers & blessings for your passion & labor in His formation ministry!

In Christ,

Shiraj Mahendra

1/20

YOUR QUESTIONS
OUR ANSWERS

*A Meticulous Response to
Fifteen Outstanding Questions
Commonly Posed By Hindus
To Christians*

PREMRAJ DHARMANANDA

FISHERS FOR CHRIST

Your Questions – Our Answers (Vol. I):
*A meticulous response to fifteen outstanding questions
commonly posed by Hindus to Christians.*

*First published in 2003 by the author
(English and Hindi versions in one book)*

Second Edition, 2017

*ISBN-13: 978-1544055558
ISBN-10: 1544055552*

*Designed and Published by
Shivraj K. Mahendra for Fishers for Christ
Email: fishers4christ2015@gmail.com*

CONTENTS

PREFACE

Your Questions Our Answers is a highly useful book, a timely gift for all who are interested in interreligious dialogue with special reference to Hindu-Christian engaging points.

The uniqueness of this publication is to be seen in that it provides simple yet profound answers to tough questions. In fact, it is filled with a light of divine knowledge that disperses the darkness of ignorance and confusion. It puts an end to superstition and doubt and strengthens a person's sincere faith in the Lord Jesus Christ.

I greatly appreciate Shri Premraj Dharmananda for this excellent work. I pray that the reader of this book will be immensely blessed!

Shivraj Mahendra

QUESTION 1

Why do Christians insist that we must reject our own national gods and embrace a foreign god? Why don't you worship God as Jesus and let us worship God as Shiva or Rama?

Answer: One of the most basic truths about the true and living God is that He is the God of all nations and all peoples. Psalms 24:1 says that "the earth is the Lord's and the fullness thereof, the world and all they who dwell therein." If Rama is the true and living God then Rama must be sovereign over the entire universe, not just India. If Jesus is the true and living God then Jesus must be sovereign over the entire universe and not just America or Britain. The reason some Hindus and Muslims think that Jesus is a national god of America is because they associate the Christian religion with the Western world.

There are several basic points which should dispel this false notion. First, the overwhelming majority of Christians in the world today belong to non-white, non-western cultures. Africa and Latin America and even Asia have vast Christian populations. Africa, for example, is the home to over 390 million Christians! Second, Christianity has been present in India far longer than it has been present in the Western world. Many Indians falsely believe that Christianity was brought to India by the 19th century western missionary movement. This is not true. Christianity has been in India since the very first century! One of the original disciples of Jesus and an eye witness of the resurrection of Jesus named Thomas brought the gospel to India in 52A.D. In contrast, Christianity did not reach N. America until the late 15th century. This means that Christianity has been in India for over a thousand years before it ever came to America. Christianity is neither eastern nor western. Jesus does not belong to India or to America. Jesus is Lord over the entire world! The message of Jesus Christ is for all peoples. Jesus paid the price for Indian sins every bit as much as he paid the price for the sins of the Americans or the Chinese or the Germans.

Third, being an Indian or a German or a Chinese is in a totally different category from being a Christian or a Muslim or a Hindu. The well-known Bengali Brahmin Brahmabandhav Upadhyay, one of the pioneers of the Indian nationalistic movement, repeatedly made the point that being an Indian is in a totally different category than being a Christian. He pointed out how absurd it would be for someone to say that a German would somehow cease to be a German by becoming a Buddhist. In the same way, an Indian does not cease to be an Indian by becoming a Christian, since nationality and religious affiliation are completely separate. Thus, becoming a Christian or not is fundamentally not a question of nationality or race, but a matter of faith in Jesus Christ. To quote the famous line from the Bengali Christian Conference issued in the early

19th century: "We have become Christians, but we have not discarded our nationality.[1]"

However, the fact that our faith in Jesus Christ does not require us to deny our nationality or embrace Western values, it is not because Indian nationality or any other nationality is greater than, or has a priority over Christianity. Rather, it is because faith in Jesus Christ *transcends* all national boundaries and encompasses peoples from every tribe, language and nation. We know that at the end of time, all the kingdoms of this world will acknowledge that Jesus alone is the King of Kings and Lord of Lords. This is declared in several places in the Bible. In Revelation 11:15 the angel declares, "The kingdoms of this world have become the kingdom of our Lord and of his Christ and He will reign for ever and ever."

Likewise, another book in the Bible known as Philippians declares "that at the name of Jesus every knee shall bow, in heaven and on earth and under the earth, and every tongue confess that Jesus

---

[1] K. Baago, *Pioneers of Indigenous Christianity*. London: Curzon Press, 1975, 3.

Christ is Lord, to the glory of God the Father" (Philippians 2:10, 11). Any and all local or national gods must ultimately fall at the feet of the true and living God of the universe.

QUESTION 2

Christianity is accepted mainly by the low-caste or tribal peoples in India. Is it because Christians are not able to convince the high caste or high-class people?

Answer: It is true that in India Christianity has been mainly accepted by scheduled caste peoples, dalits and tribals rather than by those in the Brahminical community. There are two main reasons for this. First, the social advantages and privileges which are accorded to the Brahminical community and other high caste jatis in India is very great, even in modern India. It is very difficult for people anywhere in the world to give up special privileges which they hold over against other groups. It is, in fact, true that the upper class peoples in every society in the world have been less inclined to hear the good news of the Christian message than other groups. Fundamental to the acceptance of the Christian message is the recognition that one stands before God as a needy, sinful person who desperately needs God's grace and forgiveness in one's life. A person who is well fed and who enjoys a privileged position in society has great difficulty in acknowledging his need before God. This is not merely a problem for Brahmins, it has been a problem all through the history of the church, not only in India. All over the world we can observe that those who are poor and on the margins of society have been more receptive to the gospel than the rich and powerful. In fact, the New Testament makes this observation in the very first few years of the church's life:

> Brothers, think of what you were when you were called. Not many of you were wise by human standards; not may were influential; not many were of noble birth. But God has chosen the foolish things of the world to shame the wise; God chose the weak things of the world to shame the strong. He chose the lowly things of this world and the despised

things – and that things that are not – to nulli-fy the things that are, so that non one many boast before him. (I Corinthians 1:26-29)

Second, Brahmins have not responded because there has been insufficient understanding of the Brahminical world and life-view by Christians who came to India. It is important to understand the particular mindset and life understanding of any group one wishes to reach with the good news of the Christian message. The Catholic missionaries who came in the 16th and 17th centuries and the later Protestant missionaries who came in the 18th and 19th centuries had much greater experience in reaching tribal peoples and others from the lower tier of society than the high class peoples. The missionaries themselves, particularly in the 19th century Protestant movement, were from the middle to lower classes in Europe and North America and carried a lack of understanding and, in some cases, a deep mistrust of upper class peoples. The result is that there were far fewer attempts to really communicate with the upper caste peoples of India and a far greater effort was made in reaching the lower and non-caste peoples of India.

While these two reasons are important, one should not forget that God has called people from all levels of society to himself, if they would only repent of their sins and believe the good news that God has provided forgiveness and mercy through Jesus Christ. When Jesus Christ died on the cross, He did not just bear the sins of one particular community, but He died for the entire world. The Bible says,

> For God so loved the world, that He gave His only son that whoever believes in Him should not perish, but have eternal life. For God did not send His son into the world to condemn the world but to save the world through Him. (John 3:16, 17).

The universal scope has been demonstrated by God in so many ways, including the salvation of tens of thousands of Brahmins throughout the history of India. Many of these Christians who have come to Christ from Hindu background are well known

Brahmins such as Pandita Rambai, Brahmabandhav Upadhyay, Narayan V. Tilak and Nehemiah Goreh. Countless others have responded to the gospel all across the length and breadth of India from every strata and station of life. Truly, Indian Christianity is not a tiny, marginal part of the history of India. Indian Christianity is a vital part of the history of India and has touched every strata of life.

QUESTION 3

Almost all of our gods had a wife in order to promote family and society. Why did Jesus neglect this aspect of human life? Was this sinful in his sight? Did he hate the institution of marriage?

Answer: It is true that in popular Hindu religion most of the gods have wives. For example, Brahma has Sarasvati (the goddess of knowledge), Vishnu has Lakshmi (the goddess of wealth) and Siva has Parvati (the goddess of creative power). Likewise, Rama and Sita (as seen in the *Ramayana*) or Krishna and Radha (as seen in the *Gitagovinda*) are often cited as supporting and promoting family life and an idealized picture of human love. However, if one carefully reads these stories, as well as the wealth of literature which reflects on these stories, one will quickly recognize that there are many decisions made by these gods which would be destructive to family life if practiced and accepted in our society today. For example, it is Rama who repeatedly questions the faithfulness and fidelity of his wife Sita. Even though she has been pure and faithful, he has her cast into the fire to demonstrate her loyalty to him. This is, of course, the origin of the practice of *sutee* in Indian society which is now against the law. Likewise, Krishna's lofty advice to Arjuna in the Bhagavad-Gita to slay his own kinsmen or Krishna's mischievous pranks, such as stealing the clothing of the bathing *gopis* in the Puranic literature, cannot be regarded on the face as acts which should be emulated. Indeed, such acts are illegal and certainly do not promote positive family life. Even the commentators on these famous stories realize this. That is why there is an earnest attempt to draw from these stories some kind of spiritual message, rather than taking them in the natural sense. For example, the deep longing of Radha for Krishna is seen as symbolic of the devotional love of a *bhakta* towards god. Thus, the love of these gods and goddesses are intended to portray a spiritual as well as a physical message. Krishna's advice to Arjuna to slay his own family members is taken to be a spiritual lesson about the indestructibility of the atman. To an outsider who is unfamiliar with Hinduism it would be hard to accept how the erotic longings of Radha for Krishna could be given a spiritual meaning. When Krishna steals the clothes of the *gopis* while they are bathing, who would believe that it would be used to communicate a spiritual message? Yet, this is frequently done in the Hindu literature.

Thus, it should not be difficult to accept that Jesus, although celibate and unmarried, actually represents a powerful affirmation of single minded devotion to God as well as the joys of family life and intimate love. Jesus lived a life in the *sannyasin* tradition. He remained celibate and never owned even one little piece of land. Jesus once said about himself, "the foxes have holes and birds of the air have nests, but the Son of Man (one of the titles of Jesus) has no place to lay his head" (Matthew 8:20). Thus, Jesus is clearly identified with the life of single-minded devotion towards God. This is an important ideal in both the Brahminical and Bhakti traditions within Hinduism.

However, the Christian accounts of the life of Jesus, known as Gospels, are also careful to point out Jesus' commitment to family life. For example, in John's gospel the very first miracle Jesus performs was to turn water into wine at a joyous marriage party! Jesus' presence at the wedding is intended to demonstrate His affirmation of the married life. In the teachings of Jesus we find that he strongly affirms the importance of marriage and the commitment of marriage. It is Jesus who when asked about whether divorce was permitted replied as follows,

> Haven't you read that at the beginning the Creator 'made them male and female,' and said, 'For this cause a man will leave his father and mother and be united to his wife, and the two will become one flesh'? So they are no longer two, but one. Therefore what God has joined together, let man not separate (Matthew 19:4-6).

It is clear that Jesus had a very high view of marriage. Later on the Christian Bible goes on to compare marriage to Christ's love for the church for which He gave His life. The Bible says,

> Wives, submit to your husbands as to the Lord. For the husband is the head of the wife as Christ is the head of the church, his body, of which he is the Savior…Husbands, love your wives, just as Christ loved the church and gave himself up for her to make her holy…. In this same way, husbands ought to love their wives as their own bodies. He who loves his wife loves himself. After all, no one ever hated his own body, but he feeds and cares for it, just as Christ does the church (Ephesians 5:22, 23, 25, 28, 29).

Thus, even though Jesus never got married, He remains the perfect example of how husbands and wives should love, honor and respect each other. When Jesus hung upon the cross he remembered to care for his mother and asked one of the disciples to care for his mother (See John 19:26, 27).

At the end of time, the last book in the Bible (known as Revelation) pictures the entire church of Jesus Christ (true and faithful followers of Jesus Christ), as the Bride of Christ (Revelation 19:6-10). After human history is brought to a close by Jesus Christ, all of the followers of Christ will have a great wedding feast where the church will be mystically united with Jesus Christ (Revelation 21:10-27). Human marriage and family life is actually only a pointer to that great mystery. This is why Jesus also taught that there will not be any marriage in heaven: "At the resurrection people will neither marry nor be given in marriage; they will be like the angels in heaven" (Matthew 22:30). Instead, we will all together be united to Christ. Thus, Jesus' life does not discourage marriage, but reminds us that it points to an even higher reality which human marriage and family life can only point! That higher reality is, of course, God Himself. Christians believe that Jesus is not just another avatar, but is a full incarnation of God. Jesus lived as a man while remaining One with the Father in heaven. Later He

sent the Holy Spirit to empower the church for witness and acts of love in the world.

There is perfect harmony and union within the
Christian Trinity of Father, Son and Holy Spirit.
Marriage can only point to this great mystery of the
Triune God of Christian proclamation. The stories
of Hindu gods and goddesses are simply unable to
portray, foreshadow or even to contemplate these
great eternal mysteries.

QUESTION 4

There are so many divisions within Christianity, which denomination truly represents the right or genuine Christianity?

Answer: People often make the mistake of pitting one Christian denomination against another as if the church of Jesus Christ is hopelessly divided. It is true that there are hundreds of different denominations of Christianity. There are examples of painful divisions in the church which directly contradicts the prayer of our Lord, Jesus Christ who prayed a famous prayer in the New Testament known as the High Priestly Prayer. Part of that prayer is as follows: "May they (the church) be brought to complete unity to let the world know that you sent me and have loved them even as you have loved me." (John 17:23).

However, we must ask how this unity should be expressed. I do not think Jesus was referring to any kind of organizational unity whereby the entire global church would be united as one gigantic organization. I think the unity Jesus refers to is a spiritual unity whereby the church is united in a common faith in Jesus Christ, including his life, his teaching, and the true meaning of His death and resurrection. Sometimes this spiritual unity can be clouded over by other kinds of differences which form the basis of many of the different denominations. These different groups have different ideas about certain things taught in the Bible which have, at times, given rise to various groups. For example, Christian denominations differ according to various ideas about how the church should be governed, or the precise method of baptizing a new believer into the church, and so forth. These are small differences which do not detract from the basic good news of the Christian gospel.

In addition to these, there are other differences which arise because of the vast cultural differences between Christians around the world. Unlike some religious faiths which are tied to a specific culture, Christianity has flourished in a myriad of cultural contexts around the world. Christianity does not belong to any one culture, but to the world. Therefore, some differences actually reflect the beauty of cultural diversity, not any kind of embarrassing disunity.

From a global perspective, what is truly astonishing is not the many differences among various denominations, but the great unanimity of the global church of Jesus Christ. The church may disagree on many non-essentials, but the true Church of Jesus Christ is fully united on the great essential truths of the Christian faith. This is the basis of our inner, spiritual unity (not outward, organizational) and these great uniting truths are far more important than any kind of organizational or structural unity.

What are these essentials and how can churches know if they have the marks of a true church? These essential truths have been gathered together into famous summary statements or documents known as creeds. These are statements which summarize the main doctrines of the Christian Bible. A Christian creed is similar to what the Hindus have in their *adeśa* or *mahavakyas* (great utterances) which summarize great bodies of Hindu teachings. However, one should not forget that the unity of the Christian church is far greater than any so-called unity within Hinduism. Indeed, unlike Christianity, in Hinduism there are no unifying statements which all Hindus adhere to. Even such famous doctrines as karma, transmigration of souls, caste and so forth are not accepted by some Hindu groups. This is largely because Hindus do not have a common source of authority. The *arya samaj*, for example, insists that only the *Rig Veda* contains the truth. In contrast, the followers of Vedanta insist that ultimate truth is found in the Upanishads. Still other groups insist on the priority of the *Bhagavad-gita* or some collection of the *puranas* which highlights the exploits of a particular god or goddess. The result is that the diversity within Hinduism is not only organizational or structural, but there are also fundamental differences in beliefs and practices.

Two of the most famous creeds in Christianity are known as the Apostles' Creed and the Nicene Creed. These creeds are important because they are accepted by all the major branches of Christianity: Catholic, Protestant and Eastern Orthodox. The Apostles' Creed is perhaps the most ancient of all creeds. It is as follows:

> I believe in God the Father Almighty, Maker of Heaven and earth, and in Jesus Christ His Only Son our Lord. Who was conceived of the virgin Mary, suffered under Pontius Pilate, was crucified, dead and buried. The third day He rose again from the dead, He ascended into heaven and sits at the right hand of God the Father Almighty. From there he shall come to judge the living and the dead. I believe in the Holy Spirit, the holy, universal church, the communion of the saints, the forgiveness of sins, the resurrection of the body and the life everlasting. Amen.

The truths contained in this creed are commonly held by all Christians all over the world. Thus, for example, despite the many differences, all true Christians affirm the deity of Jesus Christ, the central importance of his death on the cross, His message of forgiveness, His coming again at the end of time to judge the world and to resurrect his followers to eternal life with Him. The diversity of views which sometimes divides Christians must be understood in the light of the great unifying truths which bring all Christians all over the world together. Christians can rejoice in these great truths which unite us while at the same time learn patience and grace in those areas where we do not agree. There is a famous little poem which Christians learn which summarizes the answer to this important question:

> In essentials, unity
> In non-essentials, diversity
> In all things, charity

In summary, the marks of the true church unite all Christians everywhere, the substance of which has been passed down in the creeds. The diversity of the church is seen in the various particular expressions of the church which reflect various cultural and non-essential differences within the church. Finally, in all things we should demonstrate love, which is the greatest mark of the true church. It is love which ultimately should unite all true Christians all over the world.

QUESTION 5

Why do Christians not take *prasad*?

Answer: Discussion about whether Christians have the freedom to eat *prasad* or should refrain from eating *prasad* is as old as Christianity itself. Indeed, this very issue is addressed in the Bible. The Scripture teaches that "some people are still so accustomed to idols that when they eat such food (*prasad*) they think of it as having been sacrificed to an idol, and since their conscience is weak, it is defiled. But, food does not bring us near to God; we are no worse if we do not eat, and no better if we do" (I Corinthians 8:7, 8). In short, eating food, whether ordinary daily meals or *prasad*, does not have any power to affect (positively or negatively) our relationship with God.

The difficulty comes with new or less mature Christians who do not yet realize this truth. Take, for example, someone who is a new Christian with a Hindu background. If they see a Christian eating *prasad*, their conscience may become bothered. In fact, they may become so disturbed that they may begin to doubt whether the Christian eating *prasad* is a genuine Christian. This could even cause their own faith in Jesus Christ to falter. Because of this concern, the Bible goes on to say that even though we have the freedom in Christ to take *prasad* without any fear, we should be careful that we do not do anything which causes a weaker brother to stumble. For this reason, even though Christians are free to take *prasad*, many refrain from eating *prasad*.

It is important for Hindus to realize that those Christians who refrain from *prasad* mean no disrespect to their Hindu friends. As Christians, we appreciate the warm hospitality offered by Hindus and we eagerly long for their friendship.

Even the new Christians who reject *prasad* do not do so because they do not want to be friends with their Hindu neighbors. Rather, it is based on the Christian rejection of idol worship. The Bible teaches that there is only One God and all other gods or idols are false gods and should be rejected by Christians. These new Christians believe that eating *prasad* is a sharing in or participation in that which is evil and repulsive to the Christian faith. This is based on the Biblical command which states as follows:

> Therefore, my dear friends, flee from idolatry… Consider the people of Israel: Do not those who eat the sacrifices participate in the altar? Do I mean then than a sacrifice offered to an idol is anything, or that an idol is anything? No, but the sacrifices of pagans are offered to demons, not to God, and I do not want you to be participants with demons. (I Corinthians 10:14, 18-20).

The passage clearly teaches that an idol in a temple has any reality or power over us as Christians. However, if a Christian still fears the power of the demonic spirits which are associated with idol worship and with the offerings made to the idols, then they should refrain from eating. Mature Christians recognize their freedom to eat or not to eat, but often exercise their freedom not to eat for the sake of the weaker Christian. We sincerely hope that this sensitivity towards new Christians (or even future Christians among the Hindus) does not adversely affect any of our relationships which we enjoy with our Hindu friends.

QUESTION 6

If Jesus was God, why didn't he save his own life?

Answer: The Scripture itself clearly answers this question. When Jesus was in the Garden of Gethsemane the last night of his life, a group of soldiers arrived to arrest him. This was the beginning of his passion which culminated in his crucifixion the next day. One of the disciples sought to defend Jesus by pulling out a sword and struck one of those in the group and actually cut his ear off. Jesus told the disciple to put his sword away. Jesus' next statement deserves to be quoted directly from the Bible:

> Do you think I cannot call on my Father, and he will at once put at my disposal more than twelve legions of angels? But how then would the Scriptures be fulfilled that say it must happen in this way? (Matthew 26:53, 54).

In other words, God the Father could very easily have saved Jesus from dying on the cross. However, if he had done so we could not have been saved from our sins. Why is this? We are all sinners and we cannot save ourselves It is because God is holy and cannot sin. Jesus was completely without sin. The Bible says, "He appeared so that He might take away our sins. And in Him there is no sin" (I John 3:5). When Jesus died on the cross, He bore all of the sins of the world. His death was paid as a satisfaction for all the sins we have ever committed. This is why Jesus prayed in the Garden of Gethsemane just prior to his arrest, 'not my will, but Thine be done." (Matthew 26:39). It was the will of God for Jesus to die so that our sins could be atoned for. However, three days later God vindicated his Son by raising Him from the dead!

QUESTION 7

Rama, Krishna and other gods when tempted or persecuted, took up arms and fought for their safety and benefit, why didn't Jesus do so?

Answer: Jesus did not take up arms because He choose instead to submit to the eternal plan of God the Father for Him to lay down his life for sinners. Jesus Himself said, "greater love has no man than this, that he lay down his life for his friends" (John 15:13). There is no greater love than that which is seen in Jesus Christ. If Jesus had resisted and fought for his own life, there would have been no sacrifice for our sins. This is an ancient principle going back to the beginning of creation. When someone sins, something has to die. The Jews as well as the Hindus of ancient times performed sacrifices so that God would forgive them of their sins. Jesus is the fulfillment of all sacrifice since He is the final sacrifice for sins and once He died, no more sacrifices are needed. The Bible says that Christ

> "did not enter heaven to offer himself again and again, the way the high priest enters the Most Holy Place every year with blood that is not his own. Then Christ would have had to suffer many times since the creation of the world. But now he has appeared once and for all at the end of the ages to do away with sin by the sacrifice of himself" (Hebrews 9:25, 26).

Indeed, Jesus willingly accepted the humiliation, rejection and even death on the cross for our sake so that we would have a final and complete sacrifice for our sins. Thus, there has never been a greater expression of love than Jesus' willingness to not defend himself, but to accept the punishment we deserved by dying on the cross for us.

QUESTION 8

Should I worship Jesus Christ and follow Him even if my parents insist that I remain a Hindu?

Answer: Jesus was born, grew up and taught all of his life in the Eastern world. He was very familiar with Eastern customs which encourage close family relationships. On the one hand, Jesus taught that we should love, honor and obey our parents as a sign of respect to them. On the other hand, Jesus was also aware that some people would put their families before God and even use family obligations as an excuse for not wholeheartedly following after the living God. Therefore, Jesus' teaching demonstrates a wonderful balance between a high priority placed on honoring and respecting our parents, but always giving the Lordship of Jesus Christ our greatest commitment. This will inevitably involve painful times when our commitment to Jesus Christ may cause us to go against our parent's wishes. If such a situation arises we must follow Jesus Christ, even if our parents do not give us their blessing. Jesus said, "anyone who loves his father or mother more than me is not worthy of me" (Matthew 10:37).

Jesus said, "Do you think I came to bring peace on earth? No, I tell you, but division. From now on there will be five in one family divided against each other, three against two and two against three. They will be divided, father against son and son against father, mother against daughter and daughter against mother, mother-in-law against daughter-in-law and daughter-in-law against mother-in-law."

This passage is not referring to political or regional divisions such as exists between India and Pakistan. This passage is referring to the inevitable divisions between those who accept Jesus Christ as Lord and those who do not. This is Jesus' way of reminding his followers that devotion to Him is more important than any other relationship in the world. Jesus is not promoting or encouraging conflict, but he is merely acknowledging that His divine claims and Lordship will scandalize and divide people. This is important for those of us in India because in our society the family is extremely important.

We have been trained since childhood to honor our parents and not do anything which might disappoint them or make them angry with us. However, following Jesus Christ as Lord and Savior may very well cause our family and friends to be angry with us because they do not understand that Jesus came to save people from all over the world, including India. The passage quoted above reminds us that, while family obligations are important, following Jesus is even more important. If we have to choose between following Christ and disappointing our parents, we should wholeheartedly follow Christ.

Jesus Christ is our supreme model and in following him we will be able to fully love our friends. God's love enables us to love not only God and our dear ones but also our enemies. Thus by loving Jesus we are not limited to our family but are able to love whole humanity.

QUESTION 9

You worship Christ, we worship Krishna, why can't you worship Christ and we worship Krishna. We believe that God has come to earth at many times and in many ways to reveal Himself and to help us. Why do you insist that he only came to earth once? If he came once, why could he not come at other times?

Answer: The incarnation of God in Jesus Christ is a unique event in the history of the world and cannot be compared to the innumerable avatars of Hindu gods and goddesses. There are three main reasons why a Hindu avatar cannot be compared with the Christian proclamation of the incarnation. First, an incarnation is a unique event and, by definition, can never be repeated. The Scripture declares that "the Word became flesh and dwelt among us" (John

1:14). It is not something which was done and then later undone and which, in time, could be repeated again. The doctrine of the incarnation insists that in Jesus Christ God became a man without ceasing to be God. Jesus Christ is forever the God-Man, fully God and fully man. Even now, He sits on the right hand of the Father in heaven as the God-Man. After Jesus was resurrected, He did not cease to be the God-Man, it is an everlasting reality. In contrast, avatars are temporary manifestations of the divine and once the mission of the avatar is completed, the humanity of the avatar ceases to exist. This allows for multiple avatars from time to time in accordance with the Bhagavad-Gita which declares,

> Whenever there is decay of righteousness, O Bharata, and there is exaltation of unrighteousness, then I Myself come forth. For the protection of the good, for the sake of firmly establishing righteousness, I am born from age to age. (Gita 4:7,8).

In Christianity, the incarnation of Jesus Christ is a one time event in the history of the world.

The second major reason why an avatar is different from the incarnation is that an avatar is only a partial manifestation of the divine. Avatars represent only several of the attributes of deity, whereas the incarnation is a full and complete union of the fullness of deity with the fullness of humanity. The Bible says "in Christ all the fullness of the deity lives in bodily form" (Colossians 2:9). When we meet Christ we do not meet only a few of the attributes of deity, but the fullness of God Himself who has come to save and redeem us.

The third major difference between an avatar and an incarnation is that an avatar is a partial mingling between the divine nature of a so-called Hindu god such as Visnu with a human nature as seen in such figures as Rama or Krishna. Christians do not believe it is possible for the divine and human natures to mingle or coalesce into one another. We believe that the two natures – divine and human – remain distinct even though they were united in the person of Jesus Christ. Christians believe that Jesus Christ has two natures – one divine and one human

– but the two natures were united in the one person, Jesus Christ.

When Jesus came he died on the cross for our sins and completed once and for all everything that is necessary for our salvation. There is no need, nor any benefit from a second or third visit of God to the human race. By dying on the cross for our sins, Jesus has paid the penalty once and for all.

QUESTION 10

Why did God choose only Jesus Christ for the salvation of the world, why not Rama or Krishna or someone else?

Answer: Before we can answer this question, we need to ask another more basic question first. On what basis would God choose *anybody* to save or redeem the world? In other words, what qualifies someone to save the world from sin and bondage? Obviously, the one chosen must be someone who is himself not caught in the bondage of sin. Let me use an illustration from everyday life. Suppose someone is drowning in a lake and they cry out for help, but the only people who can hear the cries for help are themselves drowning in the lake. There is no use crying out to someone for help if they themselves are in just as desperate a condition as you are. In the same way, only someone without sin can save sinners. Is there anyone in the entire world, whether in India or in some other country who is without sin? Can any of the great gurus of India or great philosophers of ancient Greece claim to be without sin? No! The Bible says that "all have sinned and fall short of the glory of God" (Romans 3:23). The Jewish Scriptures make the same observation when they declare that "the Lord looks down from heaven on the sons of men to see if there are any who understand, any who seek God. All have turned aside, they have together become corrupt; there is no one who does good, not even one" (Psalms 14:2, 3). Even King Solomon, widely regarded by the ancient world as the wisest man who ever lived said, "there is no one who does not sin" (2 Chronicles 6:36). To put it bluntly, the entire human race is drowning in the sea of human sinfulness and there is no one who is able to deliver us. That is the first and most basic lesson of human life: we cannot save ourselves and we have no power to save another.

The sinfulness of the human race is also testified to throughout the Vedas. Even a casual reading of this most sacred text of the Hindus will reveal that the deep realization of our sinfulness and our need to be delivered from sin is regularly recorded in the Vedic material. It is in the Vedas that the ancient rishis cried out, "wipe out all of our sins" (Rg I.34.11) and the well known prayer, "remove the sin that makes us stray and wander!" (Rg I.189.1). The Vedas even acknowledges that sin is a universal condition present in the human race: "If we, men as we are, have sinned against the gods through want of thought, in weakness, or through insolence, absolve us from the guilt and make us free from sin… (Rg.IV.54.3). Furthermore, the Vedas acknowledge that God alone has the power to judge us for our sins. Rigveda declares "Thou art sin's true avenger, Brahmanaspati" (II.23.11). Sin is a bondage which has trapped the entire human race. When the Vedic rishi cried out for God to "loose me from sin as from a band that binds me" (Rg. 2.28.5) it could have easily been my prayer or yours, for this is the universal cry of the human heart. The real question which we must face is not whether or not the human race needs deliverance from sin, but whether any of the gods or goddesses of Hinduism can claim to be without sin and thereby qualify to save or redeem others from their sins. To put it another way, the Bible and the Vedas agrees that we are all drowning in the ocean of sin – the question is whether the gods of Hinduism are on the banks ready to save us or whether they, too, are drowning in sin and cannot even save themselves. Let's look at a few examples of the greatest gods in Hinduism and see if any lived a sinless life or even claimed to be without sin.

Rama is one of the great epic heroes of India. We can be inspired by the faithfulness of Sita to Rama, even in the face of his constant doubts. We can learn a great deal from Hanuman's determination to help Rama. When Rama needed a special herb which only grew on a certain mountain and Hanuman couldn't be sure which was the right herb, he decided to bring the entire mountain to Rama! This is an inspiring story. What about the stories of Krishna? Who cannot allow themselves to smile at the thought of the young Krishna as the butter thief. Many of us can picture in our mind an image of Krishna as a young child, with one hand in a butter dish and his face mischievously smeared with butter. Others may think of Krishna dancing in a circle with the gopis, or sitting by the river with Radha playing his flute or herding cows. Others see him standing majestically in the chariot with Arjuna. However, while appreciating that many of these stories have enriched Indian culture, it is hard to read these stories and come away with the conclusion that Rama or Krishna is without sin! These figures are often given over to sinful desires or they do things which are evil. The *Srimad Bhagavatam* (10:22:1-28 and 10:90:27-44; 11:1:1-4; 11:30:1-25) records Krishna seducing the gopis and even slaughtering his own children! This testimony alone should satisfy us that even the most exalted of Hindu avatars are not without sin. In fact, none of the

Hindu gods or goddesses ever claimed to be without sin.

The truth is, only the one true and living God is without sin. Therefore, only God has the power to save and deliver us. The Bible teaches that "God so loved the world that he sent his one and only Son that whosoever believes in Him shall not perish but have everlasting life" (John 3:16). Christ came, not to destroy, but to save and redeem. Christ lived a sinless life because He was truly God in human flesh. According to all the accounts of Jesus' life, he lived a sinless life and did so precisely because He was the very incarnation of the living God. That is why the Bible declares, "in Christ, all the fullness of the deity dwelt in Him in bodily form" (Col. 2:9).

Not only did Jesus live a sinless life but He repeatedly claimed to have a unique relationship with His heavenly Father. Jesus once said, "I am the Father are One." If you have seen me you have seen the Father. In another place Jesus boldly declared that salvation could only be achieved through him. Jesus said, "I am the way, the truth and the Life, no one comes to the Father except through me!" (John 14:6). These claims of Jesus were further verified by God Himself by raising Jesus from the dead. No one else has been victorious over the grave. Krishna and Rama, lie dead in the grave. Some may claim that Krishna is in heaven, but is their any proof of this? Jesus Christ, on the other hand, was raised from the dead and was seen by hundreds of eye-witnesses. One of the eye-witnesses to the Resurrection was a man named Peter, a close disciple of Jesus. In the Bible, Peter declared his testimony as follows: "You disowned the Holy and Righteous One... you killed the author of life, but God raised him from the dead. We are witnesses of this." (Acts 3:15). Thus, the crucial difference between Jesus Christ and all the avatars of Hinduism is that Jesus alone was without sin and God vindicated Jesus' claim to be the one and only Son of God by raising Him from the dead. Jesus is the Risen Lord! Someday every knee will bow and every tongue confess that Jesus Christ is Lord of all.

QUESTION 11

We hear some Christians praying to God and some praying to Jesus. Are they praying to two different gods or to the same God?

Answer: Christians believe in one God. It is, therefore, impossible for a Christian to address 'Jesus' without addressing 'God' or 'God' without addressing 'Jesus.' Whenever a Christian addresses any member of the Trinity (Father, Son and Holy Spirit), he or she is addressing God in His fullness. There is a natural logic to pray to the Father, in the Name of Jesus, through the power of the Holy Spirit. Indeed, even if our language is not that precise, this is the reality behind all true Christian prayer: All members of the Trinity are invoked in Christian prayer because we only believe in One God. The

Christian doctrine of the Trinity does not teach that Christians believe in three Gods, but rather that the one God has three internal distinctions just as the reader of this pamphlet is one person, but has distinctions of body, mind and speech.

The reason that many Christians pray to Jesus is to acknowledge that Jesus is the only mediator between man and the Father (I Timothy 2:5). However, because the Christian Scriptures acknowledge the deity of all members of the Trinity (Father, Son and Holy Spirit) the Bible refers to all members as God. Thus, the simple answer to the question is that praying to God always involves all members of the Trinity, so whether Christians pray to Jesus or to the Father, they are praying to the same God.

QUESTION **12**

Are Christians paid to bring the gospel to India? Also, aren't some Hindus paid money to convert to Christian religion?

Answer: The gospel of Jesus Christ cannot be bought or sold, as it is the free gift of God. Anyone who preaches the gospel for money is a fraud and not a true minister of the Christian gospel. Nevertheless, the Bible does permit people who spend their lives promoting the gospel to be supported by others in the church.

There are certain people who have been particularly called and gifted by God to communicate the gospel. They are excellent communicators and the church has recognized that God has gifted them for this particular ministry. Most Christian groups have a process which recognizes these individuals and sets them apart for full time service. This is typically called ordination. In most churches this means that once a person is ordained they will be given the special title of 'reverend' or 'pastor'. People in the church will then refer to these ordained men as, for example, Rev. Singh or Pastor Ashok.

People who are ordained can be supported by the church with a full salary to preach the gospel and to communicate the wonderful truths of God's Word, the Bible. However, (and this is very important) they are not being paid to preach the gospel, they are being paid so that they do not have to work an ordinary job and can, thereby, devote full time to that to which God has called them.

Paying someone to convert to Christianity is absolutely condemned by the Bible. In Ephesians it says, "for it is by grace you have been saved, through faith – and this not from yourselves, it is the gift of God – not by works, so that no one can boast" (Ephesians 2:9, 10). If someone is paid to convert, it is a direct subversion of the Biblical promise that salvation is a gift from God and cannot be bought or sold or coerced in any way.

Sometimes, when people see Hindus who have converted to Christianity prospering and living successful lives, they have assumed that someone must be paying them money. On the contrary, when we were living apart from Jesus Christ, much money was wasted on idolatrous puja, or the purchase of dead idols, or drinking alcohol or other kinds of waste. Now, the power of Jesus Christ has delivered us from all of this senseless waste of money. The result is that people's social status often rises. Money which once went to idols, now is spent building better schools and medical clinics. Health care improves, child mortality decreases, literacy rates rise. All of this happens, not because people are paid to become Christians, but simply because God blesses the lives of people who live righteous lives before Him. In Christ, there is no need to waste money on false idols.

In Christ, there is no more low caste or high caste or out-caste – all are one in Jesus Christ. These new realities make real differences in the lives of people. Jesus once said, "the thief comes only to kill, steal and destroy, but I have come to give life and to give it more abundantly" (John 10:10). How thrilling that God has given us so many wonderful promises!

QUESTION 13

Why do you insist that Jesus is the "only way" to God? Just as the many rivers lead to the same ocean, so the many religions lead to the same God?

Answer: Although this is a popular statement in India, a closer examination will reveal that it is based on sheer nonsense and not clear-headed thinking. If you are standing on a train platform in Mumbai and you want to purchase a ticket to travel to Delhi it would be sheer nonsense for the station manager to sell you any ticket available based on the false belief that "all trains lead to Delhi." The fact is, all trains do not lead to Delhi. If you want to travel to Delhi and you are given a ticket to Trivandrum, then when you arrive you will be even farther from Delhi than when you started.

The assumption that all roads lead to God just as the many rivers leads to the ocean assumes that no one really knows for sure where God is. It would be as if no one had any idea where Delhi was and so you purchased any ticket you could find and just hoped that it would lead you to Delhi. It reminds me of the famous story about the five blind men from Savatthi who were asked to describe (i.e. articulate truth-claims about) an elephant. The problem is that one grabs the tail, the other a leg, the other reaches out and feels the elephant's side, the other and ear and the fifth, the tusk. Each, because he was blind and could not see the other four, began to explain to the others the attributes of an elephant. The one who grabbed the tail insisted that the elephant was like a rope. The one who grabbed the leg was certain that an elephant was not like a rope, but a tree. The one who was feeling the side of the elephant was convinced that an elephant is like a broad, mud-baked wall. The fourth blind man, feeling the ear, was shocked that the others could not understand that the elephant is like a banana leaf. The fifth denounced them all as he held on to the tusk, insisting that an elephant is like a brandished sword. The famous branch of Hindu philosophy known as Advaita Vedanta insists that this story illustrates that even though the various paths may seem contradictory, they all point to some common goal. Hindus, for example, may be like those feeling the elephant's tail and Christians, may be like the one who says that an elephant is a large, mud-baked wall. According to advaita Vedanta, both are wrong (if they claim to hold the exclusive, final truth about an elephant), but both are also right since they do hold one aspect which is true. In this way, Hindus often explain how contradictory claims can somehow be all ultimately true.

However, as with the man who jumps on any train hoping to get to Delhi, there are some serious flaws with this famous Indian story. The whole story assumes that it is, in fact, an elephant and not a kitten or some other animal that is being described with accurate, albeit incomplete, language. Upon what basis do we know for certain that it is an elephant that the blind men are seeking to describe? The whole story is built on the assumption that there really is an elephant and at least fragmentary knowledge about the elephant is attainable. But from where does such knowledge of the 'whole' elephant come? One can only claim that each of the religions is partially true if one understands the whole. Where do we get such knowledge of the whole? In fact, the whole analogy is flawed because there are actually *six* men in the famous parable, not five. The sixth is, obviously, the clear-eyed narrator of the story who is objectively observing the five men and who sees the entire elephant and how the men are blindly experiencing only a part of the whole. Classical Hinduism has no basis for telling us where this 'sixth' man comes from. Christianity, in contrast, believes that there is a basis for revelation. God has personally revealed His Word, the

Bible, to us to help us to know the truth and to enter into a personal relationship with Him.

We do not need to just hop on any "train" and hope it will get us to Delhi, we have the revelation from God that if anyone trusts in Jesus Christ, they will be forgiven and stand blameless before the Father in heaven on the day of judgment.

QUESTION 14

How can the suffering of Jesus which took place over 2,000 years ago possibly affect someone today? How can Jesus take away the sins of someone before they are even born and before they commit even the first sin?

Answer: One of the principal problems with the Hindu doctrine of karma is that it makes all suffering the result of one's own actions, whether in this life or a previous life. In classical Hinduism there is no doctrine of vicarious suffering, i.e. no one suffers for another, they only suffer for their own sins. Thus, even if a woman is married to a man who is a drunkard and who beats her every night when he comes home and even if he gambles away everything he earns, leaving his own children destitute, the suffering of the family, according to the doctrine of karma, is not because of anything the man has done. Rather, they are suffering because of their own previous acts of karma which have embedded them in the Hindu wheel of samsara. However, most people who think about it will recognize that our actions do affect those around us. If I live a honest and godly life, it will have a positive affect on those around me. If I live as a gambler, a womanizer and a drunkard it will, likewise, have a destructive affect on those who are closest to me.

Let's take an example about someone you may never have met. The tireless laborers and writings and speeches of Mahatma Gandhi not only changed Gandhi, but the entire Indian nation today benefits from his example and his aspirations for an independent Indian nation. Even though the vast majority of Indians have never even met Gandhi and were, in fact, born after his tragic assassination, we nevertheless have benefited positively because of his life.

The suffering of Jesus on the cross is an extension of this basic principle. The Christian faith declares that God is a relational God, i.e. He created us to be in relationship with Him and with one another. Our actions do affect one another. Jesus' death on the cross is the greatest act of vicarious suffering in the world. The Bible tells us that Jesus died for the sins of the world. That means that when He died, He took upon Himself all of the sins of the world. He became the sacrifice for our sins. This means that Jesus' death nearly 2000 years ago can have a positive effect upon us. If we trust in Him, then God will forgive us of our sins. Because God is holy, He cannot simply forgive sins without some penalty being exacted. Jesus paid the penalty in full and thereby opens the door of salvation for us. Thus, the death of Jesus is not only a great example (as in the life of Mahatma Gandhi), but Jesus' death provides the actual payment for our sins so that God will accept the suffering and punishment of Jesus in place of the punishment which we deserve.

What a contrast there is between the mercy and grace found in Christ's death and the injustice in the Hindu doctrine of karma. This can be illustrated through a simple illustration. Suppose a school-boy gets caught doing something wrong which the headmaster decides deserves punishment. The boy is taken out into the schoolyard before all of the other children to be spanked by the headmaster. The schoolmaster explains to everyone what the boy did and why he is being punished and he leans over to spank the boy. However, before the headmaster spanks the boy someone stops the punishment and gives an injection to the boy which magically makes him forget whatever he did to deserve the punishment. Likewise, the person gives the same injection to all the gathered children as well as to the headmaster himself so that no one has any idea what the school-boy did or why he was being punished. The poor school-boy is then whipped by the headmaster without any knowledge of his misdeeds. This, in essence, is the Hindu doctrine of karma. According to Hinduism, we are all being punished for deeds in our past lives, but we have no idea what those misdeeds were or why, specifically, we are being punished in this life. Our current birth has made us forget all of our past births. Yet, this is not just. Everyone knows that justice involves not only punishment, but a clear statement to the accused as to why he is being punished and a clear knowledge of what crime he has committed.

In contrast, the Christian Bible teaches that "it is appointed once for every person to die." In other words, we do not have hundreds of lives to live, but only one life to live. We are guilty because of the sins we have committed in this life that we are now living, not dozens of other lifetimes which we cannot even remember.

QUESTION 15

What is the difference between Hindu *moksa* and Christian salvation? Aren't they simply two different words for the same reality?

Answer: Hindu *moksa* and Christian salvation are two very different ideas. There are three main differences between the two doctrines. First, Hindu *moksa* refers to a 'release' or 'liberation' from the ever-turning wheel of existence known as samsara. According to Hinduism, the karma which we have accrued in previous lifetimes as well as the karmic debt which we are currently accruing has trapped us into a never-ending cycle of birth and re-birth. The various schools and practices of Hinduism advocate a wide range of practices, both religious and social in order to eliminate karmic debt. The beliefs and practices vary considerably including such things as maintaining caste, avoiding certain foods or engaging in specialized learning (such as the study of the Vedas or Upanishads) or activities (pilgrimage to a holy site, dipping in the Ganges river, bhakti worship of a particular god etc...). Hindus teach that if someone earnestly follows these things, it will result in the satisfaction of karmic debt and, eventually, a release from the wheel of samsara. This release from the wheel of samsara is known as *moksa* or *mukti*.

Christian salvation does not accept either the belief that we have had multiple lives or the belief in karmic debt. For the Christian, our life and existence is not a trap to be escaped from, but it is actually a special gift from God. He created this world and placed us here to enjoy the beauty of His creation and to live fruitful and productive lives. Human suffering and pain is caused by sin. Sin refers to anything we do which violates the commands of

God. The commands of God are summed up by Jesus Christ in the following statement: "love the Lord your God with all your heart, soul, mind and strength and love your neighbor as you love yourself" (Mark 12:30, 31). In Christianity, salvation is the forgiveness of this sin against a *personal* God and our neighbor, not against the *impersonal* law of karma. Salvation restores us to a fuller, more abundant life, not an escape or release from life. The life which we have in heaven after death is a continuation of the personal joy and fellowship we have with God and one another right here on earth, except that we will be delivered completely from the presence and power of sin.

The second major difference between Hindu *moksa* and Christian salvation is in what happens to us as individuals. According to the most prominent Hindu teachers, *moksa* involves being impersonally absorbed into Brahman such that our individual consciousness is lost. Even some of the *bhakta* who speak about a personal, devotional relationship with God do not believe in any ultimate distinction between God and the worshipper once *moksa* has been experienced. In Christian salvation, we affirm that we will have personal fellowship and worship of the living God. Our consciousness will not be absorbed into the divine, but we will, nevertheless, be united to him in eternal worship and adoration. Christians reject any teaching that advocates that our consciousness is lost into or absorbed into the Divine majesty of God.

The third major difference between Christian salvation and Hindu *moksa* is that *moksa* in Hinduism comes as a result of our actions (whether religious or social). In essence, we free ourselves from the bonds of karma, even if it takes us hundreds of lifetimes to accomplish this feat. In Christianity, we cannot free ourselves from sin. There are no religious acts or pilgrimages or austerities which we can undergo to deliver ourselves from the judgment of sin. We all have sinned against God and against our neighbor and there is nothing we can do to erase that. The Christian message is that it is God Himself who comes to save us when we were incapable of saving ourselves. The Bible says that "God demonstrates his own loves for us in this: while we were still sinners, Christ died for us" (Romans 5:8). God sent His own son, Jesus Christ, to die on the cross for us and to pay the penalty which we deserved for our sinfulness. He asks us each to accept what He has done by submitting to the Lordship of Jesus Christ and trusting in Him completely for our salvation. In short, Christian salvation is about His actions on our behalf, not any of our own actions to save or deliver ourselves from the bonds of karma. Salvation is based on God's grace, not our works. The entire Christian message can be summed up in the words of Jesus Himself when He said, "for this is how God loved the world – He gave his one and only Son, that whoever believes in Him should not perish, but have everlasting life" (John 3:16). That verse is the perfect summary of the true meaning of Christian salvation.

OTHER
USEFUL BOOKS

Your Questions Our Answers
(Hindi Edition)

Christianity at the Religious Roundtable
by Timothy C. Tennent.

USA: Baker, 2002.

This We Believe
by Timothy C. Tennent.

Asbury Theological Seminary, 2011.

The Acknowledge Christ of the
Indian Renaissance
by M. M. Thomas. Madras: CLS, 1970.

INVITATION

You are cordially invited
to send us your questions – simple or com-
plicated – so that we may provide you and
other seekers with authentic answers. Please
Email us at:

fishers4christ2015@gmail.com

Thank you!

Made in the
USA
Middletown, DE